Real-World STEM:
Improving
Virtual Reality

Real-World STEM: Improving Virtual Reality

John Allen

ReferencePoint Press®

San Diego, CA

© 2018 ReferencePoint Press, Inc.
Printed in the United States

For more information, contact:
ReferencePoint Press, Inc.
PO Box 27779
San Diego, CA 92198
www. ReferencePointPress.com

LIBRARY OF CONGRESS CATALOGING-IN-PUBLICATION DATA

Name: Allen, John, 1957– author.
Title: Real-World STEM: Improving Virtual Reality/by John Allen.
Description: San Diego, CA: ReferencePoint Press, Inc., 2018. | Series:
 Real-World STEM | Includes bibliographical references and index.
 Identifiers: LCCN 2017031632 (print) | LCCN 2017031878 (ebook) | ISBN
 9781682822388 (eBook) | ISBN 9781682822371 (hardback)
Subjects: LCSH: Virtual reality—Juvenile literature. | Computer
 simulation—Juvenile literature.
Classification: LCC QA76.9.V5 (ebook) | LCC QA76.9.V5 A46 2018 (print) | DDC
 006.8—dc23
LC record available at https://lccn.loc.gov/2017031632

CONTENTS

Great Engineering Achievements

1

Electrification
Vast networks of electricity provide power for the developed world.

2

Automobile
Revolutionary manufacturing practices made cars more reliable and affordable, and the automobile became the world's major mode of transportation.

3

Airplane
Flying made the world accessible, spurring globalization on a grand scale.

Water Supply and Distribution
Engineered systems prevent the spread of disease, increasing life expectancy.

4

5

Electronics
First with vacuum tubes and later with transistors, electronic circuits underlie nearly all modern technologies.

7

6

Radio and Television
These two devices dramatically changed the way the world receives information and entertainment.

Agricultural Mechanization
Numerous agricultural innovations led to a vastly larger, safer, and less costly food supply.

8

Computers
Computers are now at the heart of countless operations and systems that impact people's lives.

9

Telephone
The telephone changed the way the world communicates personally and in business.

10

Air Conditioning and Refrigeration
Beyond providing convenience, these innovations extend the shelf life of food and medicines, protect electronics, and play an important role in health care delivery.

Highways

Forty-four thousand miles of US highways enable personal travel and the wide distribution of goods.

Spacecraft

Going to outer space vastly expanded humanity's horizons and resulted in the development of more than sixty thousand new products on Earth.

Internet

The Internet provides a global information and communications system of unparalleled access.

Imaging

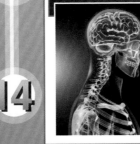

Numerous imaging tools and technologies have revolutionized medical diagnostics.

Household Appliances

These devices have eliminated many strenuous and laborious tasks.

Health Technologies

From artificial implants to the mass production of antibiotics, these technologies have led to vast health improvements.

Laser and Fiber Optics

Their applications are wide and varied, including almost simultaneous worldwide communications, noninvasive surgery, and point-of-sale scanners.

Petroleum and Petrochemical Technologies

These technologies provided the fuel that energized the twentieth century.

Nuclear Technologies

From splitting the atom came a new source of electric power.

High-Performance Materials

They are lighter, stronger, and more adaptable than ever before.

Source: Wm. A. Wulf, "Great Achievements and Grand Challenges," National Academy of Engineering, *The Bridge*, Fall/Winter 2000. www.nae.edu.

Virtual Treatment for Real Phobias

"This is what virtual reality holds out to us—the possibility of walking into the constructs of the imagination."

—Terence McKenna, American author and ethnobotanist

Quoted in Matt O'Neill, "Virtual Reality: Enhancing Reality, or Redefining It Completely?," *Medium*, August 3, 2016. https://medium.com.

For Jessica Vitkus, just the thought of peering down from a great height makes her heart begin to race. As a child, she would visit her father's skyscraper office and nervously approach the floor-to-ceiling windows as if about to plummet into the clouds. A high school trip to the Eiffel Tower in Paris led to a harrowing excursion up the hundreds of metal steps, with Vitkus shaking uncontrollably all the way. She began to regard ordinary experiences such as a visit to the Grand Canyon or even a simple rooftop party as hopeless ordeals. Yet here she is, perched high atop a rocky cliff overlooking the sea. As she swivels her head, she can peer across the horizon. She can hear the roar of the wind and the lapping of the waves on the rocks far below. With careful steps she edges onto a narrow suspension bridge, and with a shudder, prepares to step across. Then, as a final precaution, she twists the knobs on the goggles she is wearing to adjust the focus. Vitkus is actually on a platform inside a Samsung research facility. She is using virtual reality equipment to help her conquer her fear of heights. "While intellectually I know that I'm standing safely on a platform, my body still reacts like I'm up high," she says. "This is the genius part: I get to feel all the familiar feelings, and practice dealing."[1]

A Computer-Generated Environment ■

Vitkus is experiencing a digital world that appeals to her senses—or at least certain ones, like sight and hearing. This world exists only as electronic bits and bytes, yet it can seem extraordinarily real. The usual name for this technology is virtual reality. *Virtual* means "almost" or "near," and reality of course is the everyday world as human beings perceive it. This "almost reality" is a computer-generated, three-dimensional environment that a user like Vitkus can explore and interact with in real time. Interaction takes place by way of electronic equipment such as a headset or full suit. What a person knows about her or his surroundings comes from the senses and what the brain makes of sensory input. So a virtual reality device creates an alternate reality by providing a person's eyes and ears (and sometimes other senses as well) with false information that seems real. As the technology behind virtual reality improves, these made-up worlds are becoming more detailed, more vivid and lifelike, more fit for exploration—and more like the real world.

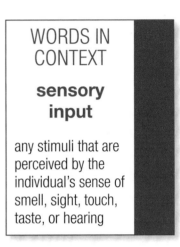

WORDS IN CONTEXT

sensory input

any stimuli that are perceived by the individual's sense of smell, sight, touch, taste, or hearing

Virtual reality has long been a staple of science fiction and fantasy. One popular example appeared on *Star Trek: The Next Generation*, a science fiction television series of the 1980s and 1990s. Members of the starship crew would relax by visiting the holodeck, a large, empty, computerized room that could be programmed to become anything from a saloon in the Old West to a tranquil field on a spring day. A darker version of virtual reality appeared in movies such as *The Lawnmower Man* and *The Matrix*. Most virtual reality plots are set far in the future, but recent advances in computer technology have made VR (as it is often called) not just a plausible fantasy but a genuine tool with all sorts of possible uses.

Practical Applications ■

Virtual reality can provide people with new experiences without the attendant hazards and costs. It enables a user to do things that are generally too dangerous, expensive, or impractical to do in everyday life. The best-known application for VR technology is gaming. VR can transport users inside an environment they previously could only view from the outside on a computer screen. Battling ogres or outmaneuvering enemy spacecraft becomes as realistic as driving a car on a crowded city street. In the same way, VR can revolutionize entertainment, thrusting viewers into a movie scene or concert stage and surrounding them with imagery and sound. Travelers could tour the Louvre in Paris, France, or descend to the bottom of the Grand Canyon in Arizona without leaving their living rooms.

Practical uses are also growing. Virtual reality systems can help train student drivers and commercial pilots. Surgeons find VR useful not only for training but also for practice on upcoming procedures, employing imaging scans to create detailed models. Designers and engineers already can don VR headsets to explore the interiors of cars and aircraft that do not yet exist. And of course, Vitkus found out how VR could be adapted to treat a common phobia like her fear of heights. As the technology improves, the possibilities seem endless.

Need for Improvement ■

Virtual reality promises to play an increasingly large role in everyday life. As with the Internet and smartphones, what once seemed a novelty could soon become a necessity in many areas. To reach its potential, however, VR technology must continue to improve. Television viewers accustomed to high-definition displays demand the same sort of vivid detail in VR output. Most VR units concentrate on sight and sound, but a true immersive experience calls for stimulation of the other senses as well. Problems some VR users have with nausea or dizziness must also be overcome.

Virtual reality has seemingly been poised for a breakthrough for almost two decades; scientists say this time the hype is not overblown and a genuine breakthrough is close at hand. Mor Naaman, associate professor of information science at Cornell Tech, predicts the rollout will be both slower and faster than some might expect. "Slower, because it will still take time to take off as a mainstream application," Naaman says. "And faster, because, once it takes off, the quality of experiences and network effects will ensure rapid adoption."[2] However long it takes, VR offers the prospect of exciting new worlds for the human mind to explore.

CHAPTER 1

CURRENT STATUS:
A Simulated World

"VR will only resonate and become part of the technological symbiosis of modern life if developers embrace it and make virtual reality at least as compelling as real reality. . . . It remains to be seen if our ability to translate imagination into executable experiences is beyond our collective capabilities, or if dense and deeply personal worlds created in VR will indeed spur the next development—not just in hardware and software, but in the relationship between humans and technology."

—Daniel Rasmus, technology strategist and industry analyst

Daniel Rasmus, "The State of Virtual Reality in 2016: What's Working, What's Not, and What's Next," GeekWire, January 16, 2016. www.geekwire.com.

Upstairs at a shopping mall in Oklahoma City, customers in special headgear look around in amazement. A teenager paints a brushstroke of bright yellow that hangs in the air in front of him. He can walk all the way around it, changing its size and shape and adding colors as he goes. A grandmother finds herself on the ocean floor amid luminous schools of fish close enough to touch, and with a shark hovering ominously in the distance. A college student wields a flamethrower as a horde of ravenous zombies descends on him. Meanwhile, dozens of visitors stand around watching these gamers and first-timers as they twitch, flinch, and recoil from the visions surrounding them. This is Upward VR, a new virtual reality arcade that gives patrons a chance to experience the latest in VR technology.

Endless Possibilities ■
Every user at Upward VR occupies a separate booth, where he or she dons a headset and grips a controller in each hand. The envi-

ronments fed to the users are also flashed on video screens outside the booths so that potential customers can get a glimpse of what awaits them. One hour in a booth costs forty-five dollars—much more than a visit to a video game parlor. Nonetheless, co-owner Will Stackable says business is brisk. State-of-the-art VR equipment like Upward VR's is much too expensive and requires too much space for most home users, so a virtual reality arcade makes sense. And Stackable is convinced the possibilities for VR are endless, especially as the technology improves. He says:

> The headset is really what sells it. When you are wearing it, and you are looking around, you are seeing what is going on within the matrix—the virtual reality world—around you. . . . There's something called presence, where there is enough sensory input your brain just flips over, and it happens so quickly. For a lot of people, it is the moment they put the headset on. Your brain tells you this is real.[3]

Stackable notes that the VR industry is expected to soar, with hardware sales, software development, and revenues from VR arcades like his predicted to reach $35 billion by 2020. "The gaming aspect is fun," says Stackable, "but this technology can transform virtually every industry there is."[4]

Upward VR and hundreds of VR arcades setting up shop around the country reflect a new excitement about virtual reality as a business venture. Sales of VR devices for home use with a game console or personal computer, while somewhat disappointing overall, have also shown promise. After years of premature hype dating to the 1990s, virtual reality seems to be finally on the verge of widespread acceptance. What is needed, experts say, is the VR version of Microsoft Windows or the iPhone. "I don't think anyone has yet developed that killer app [for VR]," says Minal Hasan, cofounder of K2 Global, a venture capital fund. "We are still several years out before we expect to see a big breakout hit on the content side."[5]

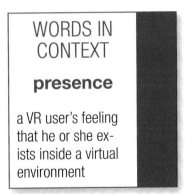

WORDS IN CONTEXT

presence

a VR user's feeling that he or she exists inside a virtual environment

Visions That Can Be Shared ■

Rapid improvements in computer technology are driving the breakthroughs in VR. At its most basic level, virtual reality relies on a simple idea: placing the user inside a digital world. Instead of simply viewing images on a screen, the VR user is immersed in an artificial, three-dimensional world and is able to interact with that environment. A computer feeds the user information that simulates sense impressions such as sight, sound, touch, smell, and even subtle feelings such as balance and position in space. It is this sensory information that creates a person's "reality." So VR can create different realities in great detail. Whereas once a made-up reality could only be described in words or shown in two-dimensional images, now it can be experienced from the inside by anyone. In this way VR offers visions that can be shared.

A virtual reality arcade attracts a young man seeking a new entertainment experience. VR arcades are popping up in cities around the world, suggesting a resurgence of interest in virtual reality technology.

As VR pioneer Jaron Lanier says, "I am still hoping VR might lead to a new level of communication between people."[6]

The idea of virtual reality dates to the 1930s, before computers existed. In 1935 Stanley G. Weinbaum wrote a short story called "Pygmalion's Spectacles" that describes an artificial reality system with goggles and attachments. It played a holographic recording of virtual stories featuring sight, hearing, smell, and touch. In the 1950s cinematographer Morton Heilig developed Sensorama, a theater booth that immersed viewers in films about dune buggies, motorcycles, and helicopters. Sensorama even had scent generators and a vibrating chair for more realism.

Today's VR began as a quest for the ultimate display in computer graphics. In 1968 American computer scientist Ivan Sutherland invented a head-mounted display system for VR. Working with his student Bob Sproull, Sutherland built a cumbersome device with a mechanical arm suspended from the lab ceiling. It was nicknamed the Sword of Damocles (from a huge mythical sword that hung over a victim's head). A user clamped on the headset attached to the mechanical arm. Inside the headset were sensors that tracked the user's head movements and gaze. A computer program displayed simple line graphics, such as a cube floating in the air, which changed position in response to the user's movements. The system was primitive, with a visual background that looked like a simple wire-frame room. Yet Sutherland proved that digital information could be used to create a virtual environment. As he wrote in a visionary essay:

> The ultimate display would, of course, be a room within which the computer can control the existence of matter. A chair displayed in such a room would be good enough to sit in. Handcuffs displayed in such a room would be confining, and a bullet displayed in such a room would be fatal. With appropriate programming such a display could literally be the Wonderland into which Alice walked.[7]

Sutherland's experiment enabled the user to view three-dimensional computer graphics while still seeing the actual surroundings of the laboratory. This led to a related field called augmented reality, in which digital graphics are overlaid on vistas of the real world.

Unmet Expectations ■

In the 1970s the US military began to experiment with 3D computer graphics in flight simulators. Head-mounted displays like Sutherland's enabled pilots to receive training in flying jet fighters without leaving the ground. Infantry personnel could prepare for dangerous combat missions, and SWAT teams could train for urban emergencies, all in a safe environment.

Research soon led to applications for the entertainment industry. Computer-generated graphics produced eye-opening special effects for movies like *Star Wars*. The 1980s saw similar three-dimensional graphics adapted for the booming video game trade. Another invention that found its way to video games was the Dataglove, brainchild of Jaron Lanier and Tom Zimmerman at Lanier's visual programming lab. This device had a computer interface that linked hand motions to a virtual environment. The National Aeronautics and Space Administration (NASA) tested

A NASA researcher exhibits a strong reaction to something she is seeing and touching in a test of a specially designed virtual reality headset and instrumented gloves. Early efforts to add a sense of touch to virtual reality systems did not always work.

the glove in its own VR experiments. Engineers at Mattel converted the idea into the Power Glove, a computerized mitt that kids used to vanquish alien foes in a Nintendo game. Like many of the first VR innovations, however, there were drawbacks. "It was cool," recalls Stephen Ellis of NASA's Ames Research Center. "But, kids quickly discovered that it's very tiring to hold your hand up in front of you long enough play an entire game."[8] Overall, VR technology, promoted as a doorway to new worlds, lacked the necessary wow factor. Computers were too slow to produce smooth graphics. Touch-feedback systems were unreliable. VR helmets were too heavy for comfortable use. And users complained of headaches and motion sickness.

Undaunted, the true believers among scientists and engineers kept on tinkering. Lanier developed an elaborate head-mounted display called the EyePhone. The entire system, including computers, sold for more than $250,000 in the late 1980s. Unfortunately, the speed of the EyePhone's headset visuals, at five or six frames per second, lagged far behind the thirty frames per second produced by televisions of the time. Nonetheless, Lanier remained convinced his visionary dreams would one day come true. In fact, it was Lanier who, in 1987, invented the term *virtual reality*— or popularized it, as some insist. The dreadlocked inventor—inspiration for the scientist in the 1992 film *The Lawnmower Man*—has continued to promote the possibilities for VR up to the present day.

By the 1990s VR seemed poised at last to become a mainstream technology. The Virtuality Group offered a number of virtual reality arcade games and machines that featured what was then cutting-edge technology. Players wore VR goggles with stereoscopic visuals—a process in which two or more photographs of the same item taken from different angles are viewed together, presenting an illusion of three-dimensional depth. In the mid-1990s Nintendo introduced Virtual Boy, a home video game console widely touted as the first portable set capable of displaying 3D graphics. However, the system was expensive;

> ## WORDS IN CONTEXT
>
> **stereoscopic**
>
> having to do with a process in which two flat images taken from slightly different angles are viewed together to create an illusion of depth and solidness

graphics were limited to red and black, causing eyestrain for many users; and the console could not be operated in a comfortable position. Virtual Boy, like other promising home VR setups at the time, proved a financial flop and soon was discontinued. "Nintendo is often blamed for poorly promoting the system, but the truth is that they promoted it brilliantly," says Dan Seitz, a technology writer. "It was just, well . . . nobody liked it. It hurt your eyes, it was clunky, it didn't feel immersive, and it just generally was poorly conceived."[9] Among dedicated tech fans and gamers, virtual reality became saddled with complaints of hype and unmet expectations. Practical VR seemed as unrealistic as the flying car.

A Breakthrough in VR ■

As it turns out, virtual reality merely had to wait for computer processors and other technologies to catch up to its original ideas. Once again the rush was on to develop a practical home system and find other functions in industry and research. Home VR development focused on two types of platforms, dubbed *mobile* and *desktop*. *Mobile* is smartphone based and allows for more movement, while *desktop* is connected to a desktop computer that is more powerful. In 2014 Facebook affirmed its faith in VR by buying a company named Oculus VR for $2 billion. Two years after the deal was announced, the company released the Oculus Rift. This VR headset, designed for desktop platforms, enables users to play amazingly immersive video games at home. The system features an affordable price and 3D graphics that are startling in their vividness. Sales showed promise from the beginning, but Facebook also saw potential uses other than gaming, such as online shopping, teleconferencing, and social networking. Filmmakers began to experiment with movies made specifically for the Rift. In October 2016 gaming leader Sony debuted the PlayStation VR for its PS4 home console, and other companies prepared to release VR systems of their own. Google even entered the field with Google Cardboard, a low-cost VR platform designed for use with a fold-out cardboard viewer, a pair of 40-mm plastic lenses, and a smartphone.

Palmer Luckey, the founder of Oculus VR, had long dreamed of creating video games that would navigate within 3D worlds. He trolled websites, yard sales, and flea markets to collect ev-

Developing Content for VR

Most developers who are creating content for virtual reality setups like the Oculus Rift have a background in computer games. But competition is growing from a new source: Hollywood. Filmmakers like Jon Favreau, the director of *Iron Man*, are excited about the possibilities that VR presents. Studio executives, who up till now have employed VR mainly for splashy demos of franchise movies, are looking into large investments to create original VR entertainments. At the Tribeca Film Festival in April 2017, the VR category—called Tribeca Immersive—featured a variety of entries. Oscar winner Kathryn Bigelow offered a gripping documentary about the work of park rangers in the Democratic Republic of the Congo who protect endangered elephants from poachers. And the VR studio Penrose won the award for best animated VR film with *Arden's Wake*, in which viewers are immersed in an oceanic world.

Doubts remain about how audiences will react to narrative VR films. Some viewers may enjoy interacting with the characters and helping determine branching plotlines, as some filmmakers hope. But who knows if audiences would prefer to wear headsets in theaters or watch VR films privately at home. Favreau, who released his own interactive VR film, *Gnomes and Goblins*, in 2016, thinks VR could have a great impact as a new storytelling medium. "Nobody quite knows what it is," he says, "but you can tell that the sauce is bubbling and something's going to happen soon."

Quoted in Ellen Gamerman, "The A-List Tackles VR," *Wall Street Journal*, April 20, 2017. www.wsj.com.

ery head-mounted VR display he could find. At age sixteen he began to work on his own headset model in his garage. Luckey raised money through crowdfunding to support his creation. The headset looked as clunky as the old versions in the 1990s, but there was a difference. "The graphics were still basic but the experience was, surprisingly, lifelike," says Matthew Schnipper, who writes for a technology website. "For the first time ever, one could casually wander through a comically realistic rendering of [sitcom comedian] Jerry Seinfeld's apartment. Or hack a zombie to death. It didn't really matter what you did inside the goggles, really, just the act of immersion was awing."[10]

The Oculus system, like those of its competitors, has benefited mainly from two things: vastly increased computing power and smartphone technologies. Computer processors now are powerful enough to create and shift high-definition images in real time, with fewer jarring pauses, flickers, and interruptions. This greatly enhances the user's illusion of being immersed in a seamless separate reality. The Oculus Rift does require a computer with a powerful video card—a printed circuit board that feeds output images to a display—something that many customers may not have and may not be able to afford. Oculus offers for download a free program that rapidly scans a gamer's computer to see if its components meet the required specs, including processing speed and memory, for the Oculus system. According to Lifewire tech expert Andy O'Donnell, "Going below these specs might result in dropped frames, motion tracking lag, and other unpleasantries that might cause VR sickness in some people, and might end up ruining your overall VR experience."[11]

Borrowing Smartphone Technology ■

Other features that have contributed to the breakthrough in VR technology come from innovations related to the smartphone. In a sense the Oculus Rift was made possible by the first iPhone. The high-resolution, mega-pixel displays used in smartphones are ideal for the razor-sharp images that virtual reality requires. A variety of sensors included in smartphones have proved essential for making VR more realistic. Sensors measure a physical quantity such as sound or distance and convert it into a signal that can trigger some function. For example, the microphone is a sound sensor—think Alexa or Siri—that can identify voices and songs.

Other smartphone sensors track motion, position, and distance in various ways. All these have been adapted for cutting-edge VR, a use the original engineers probably did not foresee. As cyberpunk author William Gibson once noted about advances in technology, "The street finds its own use for things, uses its makers never intended."[12]

The various sensors found in smartphones map the user's environment in

Wearing an Oculus Rift virtual reality headset, a user gets a taste of what it is like to fly. The newest systems are so realistic that the heart rate of users often increases during virtual reality experiences.

great detail. A proximity sensor, bouncing infrared light off the user's skin, dims a smartphone's screen when it is held against the ear. A motion sensor, called an accelerometer, keeps tabs on the phone's movements and orientation. A gyroscope adds to the motion sensor's accuracy with measurements of angular rotation. A magnetometer finds magnetic north, and a Global Positioning System chip helps plot the phone's exact location on a map. Delicate sensors in the camera lens also adjust for wide-angle views and close-ups. Light sensors can brighten the display in a dark room. A VR system like the Oculus Rift uses tracking sensors like these to communicate with the system's processing unit, telling it the user's exact position and the orientation of his or her point of view at any moment. From the perspective of a user wearing a head-mounted display, the scene will change when looking down, up, left, or right. A tilt of the head or a step backward generate a corresponding shift in the view, just as in the real world. When the update rate of sensor information is high—thanks to a powerful computer—the view shifts smoothly in real time, and the user feels immersed in an artificial world. Stereo sound keyed to the images enhances the effect. This sense of immersion, of being inside and part of a digitally created environment, is called presence. The user's awareness of his or her real surroundings falls away and is replaced by a focus on the digital experience.

Incorporating smartphone technology has also helped lower the price of commercial VR systems. With huge numbers of smartphones manufactured each year, the cost of their components has plummeted, making them more economical for VR use. "Nearly every key component in a virtual reality system—whether displays or sensors or GPUs [graphics processing units]—owes a manufacturing debt of gratitude to the smartphone," says Mark Pesce, a technology writer in Great Britain. "A VR system would still cost hundreds of thousands of dollars if we hadn't already manufactured billions of smartphones."[13]

In some VR systems, the smartphone itself is used as a component. This enables the system to make use of the sensors on the phone. For example, in Google Cardboard, a smartphone becomes the display and is placed in front of the user's eyes in a simple cardboard viewer. A VR app creates a pair of images on the phone, varied slightly between left and right for the 3D stereoscopic effect. The user then views the screen through special plastic lenses in the cardboard viewer. The images shift and react to the user's point of view and head movements, just as with a full headset. Other VR systems incorporate a smartphone into a more elaborate helmet display, but the idea is the same. Smartphone-based VR systems may not be as elegant and seamless as more elaborate devices, but they do allow users to get a fairly impressive VR experience for a much lower price.

Realistic Sensations ■

The current array of virtual reality systems is much more effective than previous versions at creating realistic sensations. A person wearing an Oculus Rift headset genuinely feels like he or she is perched on an asteroid in outer space or driving a speeding race car. Studies show that a VR user's heart rate goes up and the brain resists commands to step off a cliff or steer into a race-course wall. Although the digital characters created for VR programs are still far from lifelike in detail, users immersed in a VR environment tend to react to them as if they were real. In experiments, users grow anxious if directed to inflict pain on a virtual figure, even when the character looks more like a life-size cartoon.

A Leap into Mixed Reality

Tech fans might salivate at the thought of *Star Wars*'s lovable robots, R2-D2 and C-3PO, suddenly appearing in their living room, full-size and amazingly realistic. Such a household spectacle is in the works at Magic Leap, a company located in Plantation, Florida. Magic Leap seeks to blend computer animations with real-world imagery via a technology that game designer Graeme Devine prefers to call mixed reality, rather than augmented reality. "Mixed reality is the mixture of the real world and virtual worlds so that one understands the other," says Devine. "This creates experiences that cannot possibly happen anywhere else."

Unlike virtual reality, in which users see only the virtual world in which they are immersed, the users in mixed reality see digital imagery layered on top of their ordinary surroundings. This helps make the experience even more exciting. One game in development at Magic Leap is called *Ghost Girl*. The user begins with real wooden cubes and must figure out how to make them interact with the mixed-reality dimension. Then noises arise and become louder. As Devine describes it, "And there, in your room, is a ghost standing in front of you. . . . And there behind you is the outline of a dead body—in your house."

Engineers at Magic Leap have yet to test their version of mixed reality in the marketplace. Success or failure may depend on how comfortable users are in having their house invaded by virtual robots and ghosts.

Quoted in Dean Takahashi, "How Magic Leap's Gaming Wizard Sees the Future of Mixed Reality Games," VentureBeat, March 19, 2017. https://venturebeat.com.

As long as images stretch to the horizon and continue to flow and shift at ninety frames per second (the Oculus standard), the user generally will react as if the digital environment is real.

To experience this shudder of being in an alternate world, users must have imaginative content. One problem with today's launch of new VR systems is lack of content. It is like the early days of television, when no one knew exactly what types of programs would work best on the new sets. Users who invest in an Oculus Rift or HTC Vive system still have few choices when it comes to games and shows produced for VR. "Virtual reality is so new that much of the content that will be available this year feels more like a demo than a full-fledged product,"[14] notes technology writer Christopher Mims. To encourage content development, companies like HTC are investing millions in software firms that create virtual reality programs.

As prices come down and new content becomes available, virtual reality seems finally ready to fulfill its promise. Scientists and engineers are working on improvements that could make a VR setup as commonplace in the household as a computer or flat-screen TV. Who knows what amazing virtual worlds people will be able to explore in years to come?

CHAPTER 2

PROBLEMS: Getting a Sense of Being There

"Virtual worlds have to respond quickly enough for human users, yet need to be shared by multiple people connecting over imperfect networks. It will take a while to sort that out."

—Jaron Lanier, pioneer inventor in virtual reality

Quoted in Niall Firth, "Virtual Reality: Meet Founding Father Jaron Lanier," *New Scientist*, June 19, 2013. www.newscientist.com.

E d Hassell rushed to get the new Samsung Gear VR headset as soon as it hit the stores in his hometown of Ivanhoe, a suburb of Melbourne, Australia. Anxious to test the new technology, Hassell spent about forty-five minutes wearing the headset with no break. But almost at once he began to experience trouble with eyestrain and dizziness. The immersive sensation of VR made him forget to take a rest after thirty minutes, as manufacturers advise. Mindful of reactions like Hassell's, eye specialists are now warning that virtual reality could be hazardous to people's eyesight. Karen Makin, a senior optometrist at Bupa Optical, points out there is already evidence that VR headsets cause eyestrain and dry eyes. "There's not been a lot of research done in the field and that's the concern because it is unknown," says Makin. "Virtual reality is wonderful technology and will play a big role in our future, but the reality is that we just don't know yet what . . . impact it will have on people's eyes in the long run."[15]

Visual Conflict ■
The problem relates to a reflex that optometrists call convergence accommodation. Normally, the eyes both converge and focus on

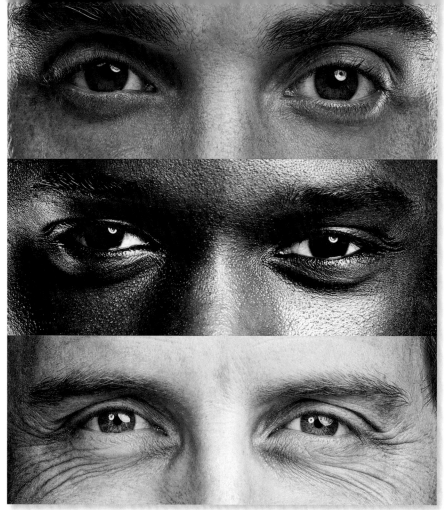

Human vision typically involves both eyes converging and focusing on the same point and the brain then processing this information. With virtual reality, the eyes focus and converge differently. This causes the brain to struggle, which can lead to eyestrain and discomfort.

the same point in space. The brain couples these two responses together as a way of dealing with standard reality. With VR, however, the eyes remain focused on a nearby screen or lens while still trying to converge on objects that suddenly appear nearby or distant. The brain struggles to resolve the discrepancy, leading to eyestrain and vision discomfort for many users. Some experts worry that VR users could suffer long-term disruptions in the convergence-accommodation reflex. However, Marty Banks, a professor of optometry and neuroscience at the University of California–Berkeley, believes long-term problems are unlikely. "Those couplings are fairly plastic," says Banks. "You can learn to change those relationships. The one you have naturally, I think you'll just go back to that when you take the headset off and look around the room and give your eyes a second to adjust."[16]

Eyestrain from this disrupted reflex is just one of the problems that virtual reality faces in its quest for widespread acceptance. Scientists note that so far, little research has been done on using VR over an extended period. Difficulties yet unknown may arise in the months and years to come. Game-changing technologies often take time before they are accepted. For now, VR developers must make improvements in certain areas if the technology is to achieve widespread adoption. First, VR must achieve true presence, so that users feel they are in an alternate world with realistic details. Second, for a more immersive experience, VR must provide not only visual information but also sensations of touch, motion, and sound. Third, people must be able to use VR without experiencing nausea or motion sickness.

Lack of Presence ■

Imagine a person strolling through a magic castle. She is opening doors to wondrous chambers filled with amazing creatures and peering out high windows onto a lush green orchard below. Suddenly, one of the doors grows dim, like a half-developed photograph, and the whole scene seems to jerk sideways for an instant. The person turns her head to look to the side, but her viewpoint sticks for a moment and does not change. Inside her VR headset, this person who was raptly exploring the castle only a moment before now feels disoriented. The wonderful illusion she was enjoying has been spoiled. Her experience ultimately lacks presence—the feeling of being inside a virtual world.

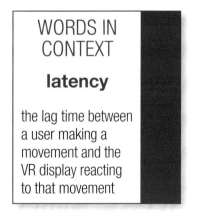

WORDS IN CONTEXT

latency

the lag time between a user making a movement and the VR display reacting to that movement

Creating this sense of presence is one of virtual reality's most difficult engineering hurdles. It involves several different aspects of VR technology, including field of view, image resolution, refresh rates, and head and eye tracking. Another problem related to the feeling of presence is latency, or the lag between the instant a user moves her head and the time that the VR display reacts to her movement and shifts accordingly. The less latency there is, the more seamless and effective the VR experience—the overall sense of being present in the VR environment. Advances in computer speeds for desktop VR setups, capable of producing ninety frames per second, have reduced latency rates and solved some of the problem. But for the highest-quality virtual reality experience, an even lower rate is necessary. As Oculus's chief scientist, Michael Abrash, explains:

> When it comes to VR and AR, latency is fundamental—if you don't have low enough latency, it's impossible to deliver good experiences, by which I mean virtual objects that your eyes and brain accept as real. . . . The key to this is that virtual objects have to stay in very nearly the same perceived real-world locations as you move; that is, they have to register as being in almost exactly the right position all the time. Being right 99 percent of the time is no good, because the occasional mis-registration is precisely the sort of thing your visual system is designed to detect, and will stick out like a sore thumb.[17]

According to Abrash, latency of as little as 50 milliseconds (ms), meaning 0.05 seconds of lag time between the user's head movement and the corresponding shift in the virtual images, produces an error that is noticeable to the user. Abrash believes a latency rate as low as 15 ms and perhaps even 7 ms is needed for an ideal VR experience. Getting there—and improving other aspects of VR in order to achieve that elusive feeling of presence—remains a huge challenge to engineers at Oculus and other VR companies.

In making the VR experience more absorbing for users, another problem is to render people, objects, and backgrounds with greater realism. Early VR setups presented people that looked like line drawings or cartoons, and furnishings and other background items also lacked detail. Today VR engineers are making strides in this area, but characters generally look softer than they should and fail to move fluidly. Backgrounds need more fine-grained detail as well as more attention to the intricacies of light and shadow. There is a long way to go before people and places in virtual reality approach the digital realism movie fans are accustomed to seeing in computer-generated imagery (CGI).

The Meaning of Presence in VR

In 2014 Michael Abrash, chief scientist for Oculus, delivered a celebrated slide presentation about the possibilities for virtual reality. At one point he explained the concept of presence.

> This feeling of being someplace real when you're in VR is well known to researchers, and is referred to as "presence," and it's presence that most distinguishes VR from 3D on a screen. Presence is distinct from immersion, which merely means that you feel surrounded by the image of the virtual world; presence means that you feel like you're *in* the virtual world.

> Trying to describe presence is bound to come up short—you can only really understand it by experiencing it—but I'll give it a shot. Presence is when, even though you know you're in a demo room and there's nothing really there, you can't help reaching out to try to touch a cube; when you automatically duck your head to avoid a pipe dangling from the ceiling; when you feel uneasy because there's a huge block hanging over you; when you're unwilling to step off a ledge. It's taking off the head-mounted display and being disoriented to find the real world there. It's more than just looking at someplace interesting; it's flipping the switch that makes you believe, deep in your lizard brain, that you *are* someplace interesting. Presence is one of the most powerful experiences you can have outside reality, precisely because it operates by engaging you along many of the same channels as reality.

Michael Abrash, "What VR Could, Should, and Almost Certainly Will Be Within Two Years," *Michael Abrash Valve* (blog), February 11, 2014. http://media.steampowered.com.

Sensing the Virtual World ■

Human beings experience the world not only through their sense of sight but via all their senses, including the senses of balance and orientation. Another challenge for VR developers is to incorporate programming for these different sense reactions to give users the feeling of experiencing VR with their entire bodies. For example, engineers are working to improve the sound inputs in

VR games and presentations. "Once the most underrated element of virtual reality, sound is now widely recognized to be a major element in creating VR with 'presence,'"[18] notes technology blogger Alex Colgan. Sound effects must be keyed to what is supposedly producing them and its virtual distance from the user. A car's engine must get louder as it approaches. The creak of a door in the corner of a room must sound like it comes from that corner. A zombie's groan must sound realistic to make the zombie come to life (so to speak).

Touch presents a major problem in creating more sophisticated VR effects. Today's VR is much improved at convincing a user's brain that virtual objects occupy real space right in front of him or her. Motion tracking devices and sensors can make virtual hands mimic the movements of real hands. The user is able to push and prod objects in the virtual environment. But when these hands touch an object, all the user feels is empty air. Lack of tactile sense—the ability to feel the hardness, texture, weight,

When VR users try to touch objects with their hands they usually feel only empty air. Tactile sense, or a sense of touch, is missing from most commercially available virtual reality technology.

and temperature of objects—is a major drawback of commercial VR technology. The ability to touch things provides a surprising amount of information about a person's surroundings, whether real or virtual. "These advanced sensory abilities are what let you locate an object in a bag amongst other objects without looking," writes a blogger on the Virtual Reality Society website. "When we consider the ways we sense the world around us and virtual reality's overall goal of replicating those experiences, it's clear that our tactile senses are a crucial component to complete the illusion."[19]

WORDS IN CONTEXT

haptics

the science of applying touch, or tactile, sensation and control to interaction with computer applications

The key to adding effects of touch to the VR experience lies with something called haptic technology. Haptics researchers use different kinds of mechanisms to simulate the sensation of touch with special gloves or exoskeletal arm coverings. The challenge is to employ things such as electric motors, pneumatic devices (operated by air under pressure), and hydraulic devices (operated by liquid under pressure) to mimic feelings of resistance, weight, and pressure. A more difficult goal is conveying various types of texture in VR using artificial means. According to experiments, perception of texture is vital to a person's emotional response to a situation. For instance, a soft toy or the touch of a loved one's hand can soothe a child, while a hard chair or bare cement floor can produce anxiety. Even further out is the possibility of haptic suits that convey sensations of full-body impact, concussive vibration, heat, and cold. For ultimate realism—think virtual spacewalk—such suits would have to include motion tracking for the entire body. Packaging all these haptic features in a commercial VR setup that does not cost a fortune will require tremendous ingenuity. Yet as virtual reality comes into its own, users will almost certainly want the ability to reach out and touch it somehow.

VR Sickness ■

Tech companies love it when young customers describe their products as "sick." However, the recent rollout of several new VR headsets revealed a troubling take on being sick. Some people reported that using a VR system actually made them nauseous. Several queasy gamers got on Twitter to air their complaints. Those who were not affected joked that new users just needed to toughen up and get their "VR legs." (This is a reference to getting one's sea legs, or becoming used to sailing without getting seasick.) But even longtime users claimed to have problems. "Can we stop talking about 'VR legs'?" tweeted one user. "They don't exist. 3 years in and bad VR gets me sick as ever, more so as I am accustomed to good VR."[20] Another tweeted, "Driveclub VR took all of 20 seconds before it made me totally sick. Never doing that again."[21] Many users have reported feeling dizzy and disoriented after an extended session of wearing a VR headset. Some users fall over after their first experience with VR. Making the transition back to ordinary reality can also cause symptoms like headache and nausea.

This effect is nothing new. It was first observed in 1957 when US Army helicopter test pilots, while training in mock cockpits with flashing screens, began to experience nausea and other symptoms. This condition, known as simulator sickness, is much like motion sickness or seasickness. (The word *nausea* comes from the Greek *naus*, which means "ship.") Scientists estimate that 25 percent to 40 percent of people suffer from motion sickness on different kinds of transport, whether planes, boats, or cars, with women slightly more susceptible than men.

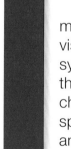

WORDS IN CONTEXT

vestibular

a system of the inner ear relating to balance or the perception of body position and movement

Motion sickness is caused by a mismatch between two body systems, the visual and the vestibular. The vestibular system is an apparatus in the inner ear that consists of fluid-filled canals and chambers lined with hair cells. It is responsible for a person's sense of balance and equilibrium. Every head movement brings a corresponding movement of the fluid in the canals. Each canal sends information to the brain on a specific type of motion, such as side to side, up or down, or angle of tilt. Normally, what a person sees corresponds exactly to the body's actual position and sense of balance. But in VR the eyes see movement inside a virtual world—diving from a

A Cautionary Tale from the 1990s

Older techies draw endless lessons from the well-known failure of Nintendo's Virtual Boy VR system of the mid-1990s. Among the Virtual Boy's shortcomings was a problem that today's VR developers are struggling to solve: nausea from spending too much time wearing the headset. After only a few minutes of playing *Mario's Tennis* or *Nester's Funky Bowling*, a Virtual Boy user often experienced a headache and feelings of queasiness. The system's display, with its red images on a black background, tended to appear blurry after a short time. "The 3-D effects are hard to focus and they strain your eyes," complained James Rolfe, one of Virtual Boy's first reviewers. "There's even a warning on the box that said it could cause headaches and seizures. That's great, right . . . how'd you like to play bad games and have a headache too?"

The problems went beyond bugs to be worked out. For example, Nintendo advised children under seven to avoid the system because of the possibility of developing lazy eye. The Virtual Boy console included a timer that reset in fifteen-minute intervals to remind users to pause and rest their eyes. Playing without a break could result in eyestrain, nausea, and neck pain from the user's awkward position leaning toward the game console. New product-liability statutes in Japan required Nintendo to post warnings about these and other health hazards. Today's developers would do well to examine the Virtual Boy saga as an example of what not to do in rolling out a new VR system.

Quoted in Molly Vincent, "What Did Virtual Boy's Failure Teach Us About Virtual Reality?," *There Is Only R*, August 17, 2016. https://thereisonlyr.com.

cliff or hurtling along on a roller coaster—while the vestibular system realizes there is no actual movement. "That gives you a cue conflict,"[22] says Bas Rokers, a visual neuroscientist at the University of Wisconsin–Madison.

In this way a VR environment, similar to the unpredictable pitching of a ship's cabin, creates a disconnect between the two systems—and the larger the mismatch, the worse the nausea. The result is a queasy, disorienting sensation. This also occurs when there is the slightest lag between the user's eye or head movements and the corresponding VR visuals. If they are not perfectly in sync, motion sickness can result.

A Hangover Effect ■

A related problem that some users have experienced is a feeling of continuing motion after the VR headset is removed. The user feels dizzy and nauseous, with a persistent sensation of the world bobbing up and down. This is similar to what some veteran sailors refer to as land sickness, or the reverse of seasickness. A person becomes so accustomed to disorienting motion, as on a sea voyage, that he or she cannot adjust when back on dry land. One user reports a disturbing hangover effect from VR:

> I was a huge VR devotee leading up to the Vive launch and loved every moment I spent in VR when I first got my hands on it, so I didn't think too much of it when I first stepped back out of VR and felt my world slightly wavering around me. After all, this was my first time, and maybe that's just normal. After waking up the next morning and still having this floaty sensation, I knew something was wrong.[23]

This user says the symptoms finally went away, but it took five weeks. He notes that others have reported problems that lasted anywhere from five minutes to several weeks.

No one is sure just why motion sickness causes nausea. One theory, dating to 1977, attributes this reflex to evolution and genetics. Whatever the reason, the prospect of motion sickness either during or after a VR session is likely to scare away many potential users in years to come.

CHAPTER 3

SOLUTIONS: Achieving and Maintaining Presence

"Presence is an incredibly powerful sensation, and it's unique to VR. . . . Most people find it to be kind of magical, and we think that once people have experienced presence, they'll want it badly."

—Michael Abrash, chief scientist at Oculus

Michael Abrash, "What VR Could, Should, and Almost Certainly Will Be Within Two Years," *Michael Abrash Valve* (blog), February 11, 2014. http://media.steampowered.com.

Sasa Marinkovic, a software marketer and VR expert, knows what a first-rate virtual reality experience should feel like. With a headset on, he is suddenly an agent catching his breath as he pauses on the roof of a high rise. He glances down at the busy street hundreds of feet below, instinctively sliding his toes back from the roof's edge. A flag on the rooftop next door whips and flaps in a high wind. Hearing the footsteps of his pursuers pounding up the metal stairwell to the roof, he decides his only chance is to leap across to the next rooftop. "I quickly turn back to have one final look," says Marinkovic, "and then . . . pixel-lag artifacts smudge my world. The magic is gone."[24] What moments ago felt like an extraordinary adventure has fallen prey to a homely computer glitch.

Most VR users have experienced what Marinkovic describes. In virtual reality everything depends on the feeling of presence—the sensation that one is inside a virtual world. Researchers say that presence involves three parts. Personal presence is when the user feels like he or she actually exists inside the virtual world. Social presence is when the user is able to interact with others in the virtual world, whether artificial characters or other real users. And environmental presence means the virtual world shows awareness of the user and reacts to her or him. VR that can produce all three kinds of presence without hesitations or interruptions—without that bubble-bursting glitch on the rooftop—seems achievable in the near future. According to Marinkovic, the number one rule of VR is "Don't break the presence."[25]

Widening the Field of View ■

To maintain that magical quality of presence, researchers and engineers are always looking to improve the various facets of VR technology. Since higher-quality VR equipment has been available only a short time, the problems that users encounter are only now beginning to emerge. The sense of presence when using a VR setup varies from person to person, so much more testing and input from users is needed to help scientists and engineers improve the next generation of devices. Each tweak brings VR closer to the ideal of presence and total immersion. And scientists expect the sensation of presence to grow even more powerful and vivid as the technology evolves.

To begin, a first-rate virtual reality setup requires a wide field of view (FOV). This is necessary to deliver the sensation of being surrounded by another world. Without any movement of the eyeball, the human eye perceives an FOV equal to 180 degrees. Full rotation of the eyes extends the field to 270 degrees. With a headset, the FOV also varies depending on the eyes' distance from the headset lenses, which averages about 0.4 inches (1 cm). Some users have trimmed the foam padding inside the HTC Vive headset to get their eyes closer to the lenses, which reportedly increases the FOV by almost 30 degrees. The challenge for VR engineers is to create a wider FOV that offers the user even greater immersion effects and depth of vision.

The first Oculus Rift and HTC Vive headsets offered an FOV of 110 degrees, which was much less than the normal human eye's capabilities. Most commercial headsets also have an FOV of around 100 degrees or less. These limits can give the user a binocular-like feeling of tunnel vision, peering at a square section of a larger frame, with the headset itself visible out of the corner of the eye. To counter this effect, StarVR has developed a headset with an ultrawide FOV of 210 degrees. "When demoing the headset, the company has a button they can press to bring in a silhouette which approximates the field of view of 100 degree

Field of view, a characteristic of how human beings see, is central to the success of virtual reality. Field of view refers to how far a person sees peripherally while looking straight ahead. In a person with healthy eyes, each eye has the same horizontal field of view. The field of view widens, or doubles, when both eyes are used. The area of overlap is what matters most in virtual reality because this is where humans perceive things in 3D and where most virtual reality action takes place. If headset makers can widen that field of view, they can enhance the sensation of being present and immersed in a scene. They try to accomplish this in various ways, including by adjusting lens sizes and shapes and the distance between the lens and the user's eyes.

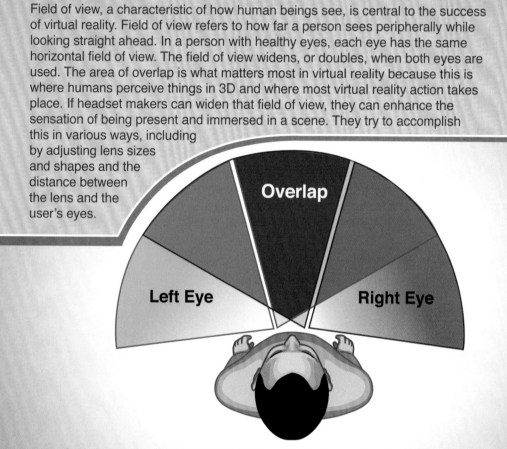

Source: Brian Ang, "Visual Field," The Gift of Sight: Vision and Eye Health. www.vision-and-eye-health.com.

headsets like the Rift and Vive," reports technology reviewer Ben Lang. "The difference is obvious and astounding."[26] Such a wide image with extra pixels—the tiny dots of illumination on a display—suffers occasionally from blurring and flickering in places, but it does provide a more immersive feeling overall. And research suggests that images on the periphery need not be as detailed as the main view in order to give a vivid impression. Some users have compared the StarVR experience to being in one's own personal IMAX theater, with panoramic images that extend all the way to the horizon.

Getting Better Resolution ◾

Another way to provide a VR experience with presence is to increase the resolution of the images. In general, higher-resolution images in VR depend on higher pixel density, or more pixels per square inch, just as with a high-definition TV. This enables the user to see sharper details, such as the sweat on a glass or the grain on a leather football. But pixel density is not the whole story. Because VR widens the FOV, software has to stretch the video image to fill the display, a feature called scaling. This results in some noticeable softening or fuzziness of the image—a quality called pixelation, in which the individual pixels can be seen. In mono video, in which both eyes see the same image, scaling can soften the image by about 20 percent, which is not a big problem. But in stereo video, each eye sees a slightly different offset image to produce a sensation of depth. Thus, two image views must be packed into each frame. The required scaling affects the image by as much as 150 percent, with 512 pixels stretched vertically to 1,280 display pixels. The result is a significant loss of resolution.

Engineers can address this problem by sending video images that have a field-of-view resolution that is a bit larger than the display resolution. When the larger image is scaled down, the resulting image has a sharper, smoother look. However, sending the larger video files necessary for this technique is a challenge for most home computers.

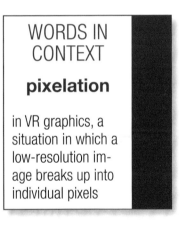

WORDS IN CONTEXT

pixelation

in VR graphics, a situation in which a low-resolution image breaks up into individual pixels

Resolution is also measured by pixels per degree (PPD), which is the number of horizontal pixels per eye divided by the approximate horizontal FOV in degrees. For example, people with 20/20 vision have a PPD of 60. The early Oculus DK1 system featured 640 pixels per eye for an FOV of 90 degrees, resulting in a disappointing PPD of 7.1. By increasing the pixel density, most high-end VR systems today offer PPDs of about 15—giving a slightly pixelated view. Experts in the field, including Michael Abrash, believe a goal of 30 PPD, providing sharper, more satisfying images, is realistic by around 2022. The key to accomplishing this is so-called foveated rendering. In this technique, the tiny part of the image that falls on the eye's fovea—a small depression in the retina that can distinguish great detail—is produced at highest quality, while the rest of the image falls away to a much-reduced sharpness (thus reducing the strain on the computer's graphics card). Nearly perfect eye tracking is necessary to locate and follow the position of the fovea, which raises an extra hurdle. With this in mind, Oculus recently purchased the Eye Tribe, a Denmark-based eye-tracking firm. Overall, when it comes to VR resolution, technicians remain optimistic. "As screens get better and better," writes Yuval Boger, who is the chief executive officer (CEO) of Sensics and blogs under the name VRGuy, "we will get increasingly closer to eye-limiting resolution in the HMD [head-mounted display] and thus to essentially photo-realistic experiences."[27]

Lowering Persistence in Display ■

Realism in VR can be sabotaged by a blurry image. One of the main causes of blurring in VR is too much persistence, or the length of time each pixel stays lit. Since the user's eye movement is much faster than that of the headset display, pixels that remain lit too long cause the image to smear across the retina as the user's head turns and the eyes move. This blurring effect, called judder, becomes more of a problem as pixel density increases. It is one of the main culprits in spoiling the feeling of presence.

Engineers address this problem by using an organic light-emitting diode (OLED) display. The OLED emits light, so it does not need a backlight to illuminate its pixels. Thinner and more efficient, this display panel has extremely low response times and extremely high refresh rates for images. With OLED, pixels switch on and off rapidly, remaining lit for 3 ms (0.03 seconds) or less, so that users see the correct scene orientation at each point as they move their head. The image appears continuous, with much less motion blur.

Achieving higher refresh rates is also vital. With lower persistence, the screen must have a high refresh rate—the rate at which frames appear—in order to avoid flickering or strobing images. Engineers have found that refresh rates of 90 Hz (90 times a second) or more are necessary to eliminate flicker. PlayStation engineers have also introduced a feature they call reprojection to boost refresh rates artificially. This method takes the last output image at 60 Hz and produces a new image at

The layered structure of an organic light-emitting diode (OLED) is depicted in this illustration. Engineers have used OLEDs to help eliminate blurring of virtual reality images.

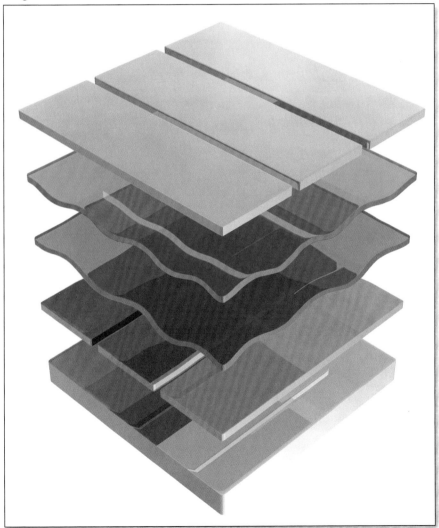

120 Hz based on the user's latest head movements. In any case, reaching much higher refresh rates for VR remains a goal for the future. For now, a powerful computer processor is required to maintain the industry-standard 90-Hz speed.

Improving Tracking Accuracy ■

Head tracking is another crucial feature for establishing presence and immersing the user in the VR environment. With head tracking, users wearing a headset see a different view when they look up, down, side to side, or at any angle. To accomplish this, VR setups use a system called 6DoF, or six degrees of freedom. This system plots the rotation of a user's head according to positions

Delivering the "Wow" Sense of Presence

The Seattle-based virtual reality company Pixvana wants to improve the quality of VR videos for all users. To that end, Pixvana has not only released a new streaming technology but also is making it available as an open standard for other companies to adopt and modify. The technology is called FOVAS, for field-of-view adaptive streaming. It improves video quality for VR while reducing its bandwidth requirements—the necessary data rate supported by the network connection—by 70 percent. FOVAS includes more pixels for a sharper image, twenty-four times the 1080-pixel resolution of high-definition TV. By making the FOV slightly larger than the display resolution, the scaled-down high-definition image looks incredibly vivid and detailed. FOVAS also supports VR presence by ensuring that the image is always sharpest in the exact area where the user is looking. "We call it 'virtual reality,' but often low resolution and harsh compression make the video look so bad that it distracts the viewer from true immersion," says Forest Key, Pixvana's cofounder and CEO. "Using FOVAS is like swapping your old standard definition set for a 4K TV. The goal is to deliver the 'wow' sense of presence to consumers that is the hallmark of VR."

Quoted in Dean Takahashi, "Pixvana Spin Player Lets You Publish and Stream High-Quality VR Videos," VentureBeat, September 29, 2016. https://venturebeat.com.

on an x-, y-, and z-axis, measuring how the head moves forward and backward, side to side, and shoulder to shoulder (also called pitch, yaw, and roll).

An inertial measurement unit made up of components based on smartphone technology, such as a gyroscope, accelerometer, and magnetometer, adds positional tracking of the headset in space to the head-tracking feature. Data from these features is then synchronized in real time to establish the user's position and orientation in the virtual world. VR headsets like the HTC Vive and Oculus Rift that are tethered to a desktop PC make use of an external device, such as a camera on the computer display, to track the position of the headset. More trackers can be added around the room to increase accuracy. This technique is known as outside-in tracking. It generally works well, but is prone to tracking problems if objects such as a couch or houseplant get in the way as the user moves around.

Many VR engineers now believe inside-out positional tracking is an even better solution. With inside-out tracking, all sensors are located on the headset itself, allowing for much greater mobility. As the user moves in the headset, the sensors constantly reco-ordinate her or his position in the room. For example, Eonite has introduced inside-out tracking software for VR that is accurate to less than 1 millimeter and has very low latency. Eonite's tracking software is based on its cofounders' work with artificial perception in robots. "It's not a future promise. It works," says Eonite CEO Youssri Helmy. "It's the same core technology for tracking robots as tracking headsets. The tech they had blew me away."[28]

Reducing Latency ■

With regard to tracking, latency is key to maintaining presence. Higher latency rates mean that the user's view does not shift smoothly as he or she moves, resulting in loss of presence and, often, dizziness and nausea. Scientists refer to the problem as motion-to-photon latency, meaning the time needed for a user's movement to be completely registered on a display screen in photons, or particles of light. Sensitivity to latency varies by individual, but today's top VR systems can lower latency in certain games to nearly 20 ms (0.02 seconds), and start-up companies are claiming latency rates of less than 5 ms (0.005 seconds).

"Maybe you don't think that a few milliseconds of latency sounds like a big deal," says VR developer E. McNeill. "But I'm willing to bet that you don't like getting sick, and these features can determine whether you feel nauseous or not."[29]

One solution that shows promise is predictive tracking. In this technique, the VR system guesses the user's next movement, and the software renders the scene one or more frames into the future in accordance with the prediction. It is like predicting where a user will be looking before the user's head is turned. Predictive tracking uses detailed analyses about how a person's head and neck rotate, along with algorithms based on position and velocity of movement. For best results, position and velocity need to be measured with great accuracy, without any measurement interference or noise. The VR system may also track movement of eyes, head, and hands differently depending on the latency of each. This allows all these types of movement to be drawn in sync with future frames in the same VR scene. In fact, eye-tracking information can be used to anticipate head movements. Predictive tracking can produce a smoother VR experience, but if the software guesses wrong, it can also result in a jarring disruption that destroys any sense of presence.

Creating Realistic People ■

A strong sense of presence is also bolstered when people and objects in the VR environment are rendered realistically. Improvements in 3D computer games and CGI graphics in films have already led users to expect characters, furnishings, and backgrounds to have a high level of detail. Advances in computer processors have helped make this possible. Textures in a VR environment such as fabrics, wood grains, and metal surfaces are presented with surprising accuracy so that the user's eye accepts them at once. And whereas characters in virtual reality used to look like wire outlines or gangly cartoons, they now typically appear much more lifelike.

For now it remains enormously expensive to create realistic people in VR. Developers typically must spend hours getting the skin textures, facial expressions, physical movements, and shadowing just right. Even then the most realistic-looking characters in VR have a certain quality of being slightly off—what the Japanese

A scientist makes adjustments on a lifelike robot. Virtual reality and robotics both suffer from the uncanny valley effect, which is a feeling of uneasiness or even revulsion when people see human replicas that seem to be slightly off.

robotics expert Masahiro Mori dubbed the uncanny valley effect. This is when human replicas that are not quite fully human-like give viewers an eerie feeling that repels them. "Creating realistic virtual humans is incredibly complex, and often can't be pulled off in the right way," says Matias Volonte of the Virtual Environments Group at the Clemson University School of Computing. "At times,

Zero Latency and Pure Immersive Mayhem

"Imagine a game that doesn't feel like a game. Where your body is the controller and your mind believes it's real. The digital and real world meshed seamlessly together, to transport you inside the virtual like never before. When you move, the game moves with you. Pure immersive mayhem with the freedom to get up and go."

This pitch can be found on the website of Zero Latency, a start-up based in Melbourne, Australia, that specializes in wireless motion-tracking technology for VR. The company name shows the emphasis it places on reducing the lag time in VR graphics display. It touts its VR games as free-roaming and has set up large game-playing spaces in Tokyo, Japan; Madrid, Spain; and Orlando, Florida, to demonstrate its wireless, free-roaming concept. The company's state-of-the-art hardware fits in a player's backpack yet is able to power robot attack and zombie outbreak games that look incredibly detailed and operate smoothly without interruptions or glitches. With space-age rifles in hand (that show up identically in the VR world), players run, crouch, and execute backflips as they join with fellow players to pursue their foes over a wide area. Zero Latency is demonstrating how immersive VR games that respond in real time can be a heady experience for gamers worldwide. Or as the company urges: "Pit yourself against undead hordes and outwit rebel raiders as you and your team race to restore order, before the clock runs out."

Zero Latency. https://zerolatencyvr.com.

it's just as well to go with a cartoonish alternative. But we need to better understand the when and why to help developers make this serious decision."[30]

Some developers are betting that improvements in VR are leading to a highly-realistic experience that includes lifelike characters. A San Francisco tech company called 8i employs multiple cameras to capture human figures from every angle in order to create virtual people that seem true to life. The idea is that VR users could walk completely around a virtual golf instructor to inspect a swing or feel what it is like to be onstage with a rock guitarist. Engineers at 8i create each VR person by filming subjects with forty high-definition cameras on a soundstage in Los Angeles. Then the company uses software to combine the footage into a detailed three-dimensional creation. Each virtual person can become an avatar, or stand-in for a VR user, in a socially interactive game or scenario. The avatars can also be used to create realistic patients for medical training. Linc Gasking, 8i's CEO and cofounder, thinks the possible applications are endless. "What we've found," he says, "is that there is really a race toward creating an incredibly realistic experience."[31]

CHAPTER 4

SOLUTIONS:
Appealing to the Senses

"You'll still want to satisfy basic sensory needs to make a virtual world truly immersive. Sight is a big one, sound is also important, but I would also include equilibrium and balance as being a high requirement. And touching things does indeed render them to be more real than anything."

—Lemuel Pew, independent game designer

Quoted in Anna Demidenko, "Why VR Is Not Full-Fledged Without Haptic Technology," *Tesla Suit* (blog), May 6, 2017. https://teslasuit.io.

A young woman playing a virtual reality game finds herself on a deserted street fleeing from a gang of bloodthirsty vampires. She turns down an alleyway and suddenly faces a high brick wall blocking her path. She reaches out to touch the wall, but her hand seems to flow right through it. So is the wall there or not? For full immersion in the game, she has to know. And for the next wave of VR to be truly immersive, many scientists and technologists believe, it must appeal to all the senses, not just sight and hearing.

Haptics for a Sense of Touch ■

A wall in a first-rate VR experience can seem impressively solid—that is, until the user tries to touch it. Now a team of researchers at the Hasso-Plattner-Institut in Potsdam, Germany, is testing a VR system that simulates walls and heavy obstacles through electrical stimulation of the user's muscles. The test subject is fitted with a backpack that contains a medical-grade eight-channel electric muscle stimulator (EMS) and a laptop running the software. The EMS is controlled by a VR system connected by a USB cable to a Samsung Gear VR headset with trackers for head and hand movements. Electrodes are attached to the user's forearms, biceps, triceps, and shoulders. When the tracker perceives that the user is touching or pushing a virtual object, the electrodes automatically deliver a mild shock (which is not dangerous or painful). This causes the activated muscle to tense, which repels the user's hand as if he or she is feeling the solid wall or pushing against it. The sensation also works with lifting heavy virtual objects. "We were really interested in trying to explore one of the hardest things to recreate in terms of physical sensation, which is a wall," says Pedro Lopes, one of the system's creators. "The major potential here is that this is something you can have with very little hardware."[32]

The team's EMS system is an example of haptic technology, which uses a controller activated by electric current, pneumatic pressure, or hydraulic pressure to mimic the application of force, pressure, or resistance to a virtual image. The use of haptics is one way developers are trying to move beyond sight and sound to include other senses in the VR experience, such as touch, balance, and body awareness. Currently, VR features like the HTC Vive wands track hand and arm motions via controllers that are held firmly in the user's palms. They work well for syncing hand motions with the VR feed but offer little in the way of conveying a

A gamer tries out the HTC Vive wands. The wands track hand and arm motions via controllers that are held firmly in the user's palms.

sense of touch. Haptic technology is crucial to creating a virtual world that can be touched and manipulated, has realistic weight and feel, and pushes back against the VR user's efforts.

Creating a realistic simulation of touching different materials was a challenge for the researchers. Their first attempts to apply a current were strictly aimed at keeping users from passing their hands through a virtual wall. But the effect was too strong, as one participant claimed it felt like a magnet jerking his hand backward. Finally, they struck the right balance in two different simulators. In one they programmed a limit for the intensity of the EMS burst that enabled the user to sink his or her hand into a virtual object by about 4 inches (10 cm). This gave the effect of pressing the hand into foam or some other soft surface. The other simulator produced a quick EMS pulse that repelled the user's hand—with a sensation like a counterforce—so it would not push through a solid object like a wall. Lopes believes this technology is only the beginning. "There's a need for physicality in VR," he says. "The next step is bigger force, more physical sensations."[33]

Haptic Feedback for the Entire Body ■

A similar approach to adding sensations of touch to VR comes from Tesla Studios, an offshoot of the cutting-edge manufacturer of electric cars. Tesla engineers have developed the Teslasuit, a full-body wearable array for haptic feedback. The suit is made of so-called smart textiles, or fabrics embedded with conductive thread that fools the senses with mild electric shocks to the neuromuscular system. By adjusting the intensity of these light zaps to various points of the body, the Teslasuit can simulate a range of physical sensations in a VR environment. "[The Tesla engineers] claim the suit is capable of producing feedback spanning everything from full body hugs, to the impact of bullets and explosions (albeit hopefully not quite as painful or life threatening)," notes technology writer Paul James. "Not only that, the suit can apparently simulate climate changes in the VR environment, [warming] the wearer to a claimed 30 degrees."[34] (That is, 30°C, or 86°F.) A suit

Haptic Skin That Feels Alive

A haptic technology that is less elaborate—and less expensive—than most current versions is Omnipulse, which is being developed by Cornell University's Organic Robotics Lab. Omnipulse makes use of a number of pneumatic actuators, or controls activated by compressed air. The haptic feedback it produces feels quite natural in comparison to some of the purely mechanical haptic systems. The flexible haptic sleeve, which feels much like skin, fits snugly over the VR hand controller, like the ones on the HTC Vive setup. Once in place it is tethered to a compressor that inflates the various actuators as the user grips the controller. For such a simple, compressed-air-based system, the Omnipulse is effective at conveying a variety of tactile sensations, such as punching things, shooting a squirt pistol, hammering a nail, and feeling the recoil of a handgun.

However, there is an aspect to the Omnipulse that some users find unnerving. When the Omnipulse unit is on, the separate pockets of the sleeve pulsate and bubble up in an odd fashion, as if something inside is trying to escape. "Combined with the roundness of the inflating pockets, the whole ordeal feels quite a bit more squishy and organic than many other haptics technologies we've used for VR," claims Ben Lang, a technology reviewer on the Road to VR website. "When you see it active on the controller when it isn't in anyone's hand, squirming and shaking the controller at times, it's actually a little creepy how it seems . . . alive."

Ben Lang, "This Pulsating 'Haptic Skin' Is Somewhat Creepy, Mostly Awesome," Road to VR, May 9, 2017. www.roadtovr.com.

that can offer a gamut of tactile sensations from hugs to gunshots could, for example, place VR spectators in the middle of a gangster movie like never before.

The Teslasuit runs on a battery contained in a T-belt. The T-belt acts as the suit's control unit, holding the system hardware and a Bluetooth radio setup that connects wirelessly to a PC. The two-piece suit's conductive thread is covered with waterproof neoprene, a flexible synthetic rubber, and is fully washable. However, at around $150,000, the prototype for now is too expensive for most people, let alone the average gamer. Industry experts also question whether the full-body technology has the backing of game developers. As VR reviewer Jamie Rigg explains:

> The product itself, the funding goal and the delivery estimates are relatively ambitious, but it's the chicken and egg problem that's the real red flag. Consumer VR is still in its embryonic infancy, and the likelihood of developers going out of their way to support the Teslasuit accessory in their games and other experiences might be a tall order, especially if there are few out in the wild. In the future, there will almost certainly be opportunities for value-adding peripherals that excite developers. Right now, though, the Teslasuit concept may be a little ahead of its time.[35]

A Virtual Surgeon's Touch ■

The prospect of adding a delicate sense of touch to VR has applications far beyond the realm of games and films. Aler Gu, a young robotics engineer from China, has helped develop a glove that can manipulate objects in the virtual world with amazing dexterity. The Dexmo glove looks bulky and clumsy, with its jet-black hand coverings and glossy, white, clawlike fingers, yet it is wireless and surprisingly light. The glove, employed with the proper VR software, enables a wearer to touch, press, and grasp objects in the virtual world as if they had all the characteristics of reality. With the Dexmo glove, a user can feel the difference between a hard brick and a soft pillow. An egg feels solid but fragile. A sponge or foam cushion in the digital world can be squeezed firmly between the oversized robotic fingers.

The Dexmo glove is the work of seven young engineers, led by Gu, at the Chinese company Dexta Robotics. The exoskeleton device features five custom-made units that loop over a person's fingertips. When the user grasps an object in a VR environment, the exoskeleton pulls back on his or her fingers, mimicking the force and resistance of gripping that particular object. "In addition to simulating how large an object in VR is, Dexmo can provide a sense of firmness by varying how abrupt the arms pull back on your fingers," says VR expert Ryan Whitwam. "For example, the handle of a sword would have very little give. But you'd experience a more gradual increase in force as you closed your hand around a virtual pillow."[36]

Tiny motors in the exoskeleton also can produce haptic vibrations in the fingertips to simulate subtle sensations like running the hand across rough cement or tapping on a keyboard. Gu believes the Dexmo glove, with its precise tactile sensations, could be used to train surgeons to perform realistic operations. The device could simulate the various levels of resistance a scalpel

Customizing VR Sound

With so much emphasis placed on visual effects in virtual reality, sound is often taken for granted. Yet this underrated aspect of VR can play a major role in establishing presence for the user. The audio in VR is used much as it is in movies, providing realistic sound effects and background sounds such as wind, street noises, echoing footsteps, and other details.

One difference with VR soundtracks is the importance of sound as a cue to guide the user's attention to certain areas of the virtual space. The creak of a hinge or the click of a pistol being cocked can attract a user's gaze like a magnet. The trick for VR engineers is to ensure a precise sense of sound localization for the individual user—meaning he or she can tell exactly where the sound is coming from. The human brain uses the subtle differences in the way a sound enters the left and right ears to process spatial location. Researchers have studied how different head shapes and sizes affect the ear's reception of a sound from a specific point in space, a concept known as head-related transfer function (HRTF). Sound engineers use HRTF data to situate individual sounds so that they are linked to spatial cues in the VR game or film. "From there, custom HRTF functions are produced for you and you only," notes VR analyst Tuan Nguyen. "Sounds are matched to your ears."

Tuan Nguyen, "True 3D Audio Based on HRTFs Is Back, and VR Needs It," *PC Gamer*, February 23, 2016. www.pcgamer.com.

would encounter with different types of tissue. It could also be used in training law enforcement and military personnel to disarm and dismantle bombs.

Gu notes that the Dexmo glove, by adding a subtler sense of touch to VR, could help maintain the user's all-important feeling of presence. "The maximum level of feedback current VR controllers give is a gentle rumble using vibration motors," says Gu. "But vibration alone isn't enough to fool the brain. The moment you detect anomalies [departures from the norm] in how objects feel, your sense of immersion is broken."[37]

Getting the Scent of Virtual Reality ■

For full immersion in VR, some scientists have dreamed of including the sense of smell in virtual reality simulations. Feelreal, a start-up company located in Brooklyn, New York, has created a piece of VR hardware that not only simulates weather effects but also provides a variety of scents. The Feelreal mask, which attaches to the bottom of a commercial VR headset like the Oculus Rift or Sony Morpheus, places the user's nose, mouth, and cheeks in range of its nozzles. Depending on the virtual scene, the mask can activate microheaters, microcoolers, and an ultrasonic ionizing unit that sprays water mists. Blasts of hot air accompany a virtual fire, and a fine mist enhances the sensation of a virtual waterfall. A small engine produces vibrations that simulate the resonance of thunder. Perhaps most unusual is the array of odor cartridges that can spritz a number of different scents into the user's nostrils. According to the company's website, the smells include jungle, ocean, fire, grass, powder, flowers, and metal, with many more selections to come. One skeptical reviewer of the Feelreal mask did enjoy some of the experience:

> I got through a grassy field and a rainforest without more than moderate discomfort. And then, for a few moments, the system worked. I was floating towards a waterfall, sun shining on the rocks around me. FEEL WET, a caption promised. The Feelreal's coolers began to chill the air around my nose and mouth, and a moment later, I felt a drop of water hit my cheek. It wasn't natural, exactly, but it was pleasant—like a cool breeze on the stuffy convention floor.[38]

Shortly thereafter, the demo shut off the microcoolers and blasted the reviewer with hot air, as if a hair dryer were aimed at her nose and mouth, giving her a sensation of smothering in a hot car. Scents and weather effects may one day become standard for VR games and films, but demand for such features seems certain to remain low for now. The Feelreal mask project has failed to secure necessary funding, and further development of the idea may be delayed for some time.

So Realistic One Can Taste It ■

Engineers also are looking at ways to convey taste in VR. For example, a gamer confronted with a sumptuous banquet scene in a virtual scenario could actually sample the flavors of the foods on display. Perhaps he or she could even enjoy the sensation of chewing the delicious, if imaginary, fare. Cutting-edge electronics may soon enable VR users to taste and chew virtual dishes even though their mouths remain empty.

The trick is to use electric current to stimulate the taste buds and other receptors on the tongue and in the mouth. In recent experiments scientists already have had success fooling subjects into tasting foods that are not really there. Nimesha Ranasinghe of the University of Singapore has tested a so-called digital lollipop that can trick the tongue with a few well-placed zaps into tasting a variety of flavors, including salty, bitter, sour, and sweet. The device, when hooked up to a laptop, employs electrical stimulation of four areas on the tongue to produce the sensation of taste.

Someday virtual reality users might actually be able to taste and smell each of the foods served during a virtual banquet. The key to this innovation lies in using electric current to stimulate taste buds and other receptors on the tongue and in the mouth.

Ranasinghe and his team have also invented an electric spoon studded with electrodes that can mimic taste reactions on the tongue. The original goal of his work was to help patients boost their ability to taste. "People with diabetes might be able to use the taste synthesizer to simulate sweet sensations without harming their actual blood sugar levels," says Ranasinghe. "Cancer patients could use it to improve or regenerate a diminished sense of taste during chemotherapy."[39]

Now Ranasinghe and others are pursuing related ideas to add taste and food texture to a user's VR experience. One project uses temperature changes to simulate a flavor of sweetness or sourness on the tongue. The VR user extends the tip of the tongue to a thermoelectric unit the size of a harmonica. As the unit rapidly heats up or cools down, thermally sensitive neurons on the tongue produce a sensation of taste. In trials, about half the participants responded to the temperature changes. Some claimed that a warming burst gave them a spicy taste and a cooler surge led to a minty flavor. Such a thermal device could theoretically help a VR user taste foods that appear on-screen.

Researchers at the University of Tokyo in Japan hope to add the experience of food texture to the VR palette. Arinobu Niijima and Takefumi Ogawa have created what they call the Electric Food Texture System to reproduce the sensations of food inside the mouth. Their device places electrodes not on the tongue but on the masseter muscle, a jaw muscle involved in chewing. Applying short pulses of current as the user bites down gives a sensation of hard, crisp, or chewy food texture. "There is no food in the mouth, but users feel as if they are chewing some food due to haptic feedback by electrical muscle stimulation,"[40]

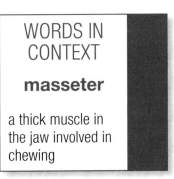

WORDS IN CONTEXT

masseter

a thick muscle in the jaw involved in chewing

says Niijima. He and Ogawa plan to target other muscles in the jaw to simulate even more subtle food textures. They are also working on adding the appropriate chewing sounds to the virtual mix.

Stimulating other senses besides sight and hearing promises to give VR users a more vivid feeling of presence in the virtual world. Although some innovations may be too expensive or elaborate to serve a wide audience, they demonstrate how science is learning to re-create the world in a digital form.

CHAPTER 5

SOLUTIONS:
Reducing Motion Sickness

"Motion sickness situations are ones in which the control of your body is challenged somehow. If you don't rise to that challenge, then the contents of your stomach may rise."

—Thomas Stoffregen, kinesiologist at the University of Minnesota–Minneapolis

Quoted in Betsy Mason, "Virtual Reality Has a Motion Sickness Problem," *Science News*, March 7, 2017. www.sciencenews.org.

The first major wave of commercial VR headsets in the 1990s created a great deal of buzz but also left many users feeling more than a little bit queasy, and with tired eyes and an aching head. When users mention that today's headsets leave them feeling less nauseated, that may not sound like much of an endorsement. But VR developers are making progress in solving the key problem, which is the brain's stubborn resistance to accepting virtual reality as something real. The brain expects the senses and the motor systems to work closely in tandem. When there is a discrepancy, the trouble starts. Technology writer Sarah Zhang notes:

> Call it motion sickness or 'simulator sickness' or 'cybersickness,' but the nausea is real and has long bedeviled virtual reality. The main reason is latency, or the tiny but perceptible delay between when you move your head in VR and when the image in front of your eyes changes—creating a mismatch between the motion we feel (with our inner ears) and the image we see (with our eyes).[41]

Another cause of motion sickness is what neuroscientists call a cue conflict. A person's eyes see movement in the virtual world, but the inner ear system knows that the body is not moving. A VR user might lean into a turn as the virtual car he or she is driving approaches a bend in the road. In reality, the person ends up on the floor feeling a bit dizzy.

No Single Solution to VR Sickness ■

So far VR developers have found no single solution to the problem of motion sickness. Their ideas tend to veer wildly between small practical tweaks to the VR system and complete overhauls that alter the way users interact with the virtual world. In general, more powerful processors and more rapid refresh rates have addressed the larger issues with latency that caused users to feel nauseous in the past. The Oculus Rift has touted its supercharged 90-Hz refresh rates, which help reduce the fatal lag time

An ear anatomy illustration shows the inner ear as the light green spiraling feature on the right. Motion sickness can result when people see themselves moving in the virtual world while the workings of the inner ear know that no movement is actually taking place.

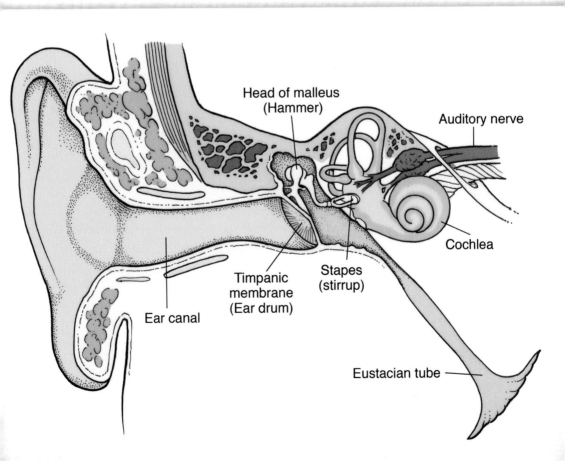

that can lead to nausea for VR players. The HTC Vive claims that its Lighthouse room tracking system can eliminate motion sickness entirely. Lighthouse tracks data points from the user's body movements with great precision in order to re-create that movement in virtual reality. When the movements are synced, the user feels more in control and is less prone to nausea and dizziness.

Still, the problem remains uppermost in the minds of many new users. Who wants to worry about getting sick while playing a game or watching a film? In any case, since motion sickness varies among individuals—with some able to tolerate a virtual rollercoaster ride and others made queasy by the first few steps in a VR headset—solutions may have to be tailored to individuals as well.

From Teleportation to Slo-Mo ◼

For example, some users feel unstable and get an upset stomach in even smoothly operating VR environments if they have to make a virtual walk from one place to another. The surrounding landscape can seem to tilt or lurch in response to a sideways glance. To deal with this problem, many games introduce so-called teleportation. Users can point to wherever they want to go in the scene, and instantly they are there. This eliminates the rocking visualization of movement, which causes the nausea. It also removes the need to fiddle with a joystick or stomp around the living room wearing a headset in order to reach a new location in the environment. Developers are finding clever ways to integrate the idea of teleportation into their games. In Epic Games's *Robo Recall*, users press a control stick to produce a blue line that flows across the scene. Users can then choose where to move along that line (the movement is instantaneous) and which direction to be facing when they arrive. Other games use teleportation in a similar way, but they often allow it only between predetermined spots.

> **WORDS IN CONTEXT**
>
> **teleportation**
>
> ability of users to point to wherever they want to go in a scene and then instantly arrive at that point

A related solution is to enable users to only move directly toward their viewpoint. This reduces the motion sickness many people experience from sideways or backward movement in the

Tips for Avoiding Motion Sickness with VR

Dozens of industry experts have suggested ways that VR users can avoid motion sickness or deal with it should it occur. Among the most frequent suggestions are the following:

- If you start to feel queasy while playing a VR game, stop, shut your eyes, breathe deeply, and take a break before you try it again.

- Eat ginger or take ginger capsules before playing. Many people have found that ginger reduces nausea.

- Take an antiemetic (antinausea) medicine.

- Have a fan blowing on yourself as you play. VR gamers in online forums report this often helps them remain more comfortable.

- Do not eat right before using VR.

- Avoid racing or roller-coaster games that involve lots of rapid movement.

- Try different FOV options to see which works best for you.

- Should you experience motion sickness, get a good night's sleep to allow your inner ears to rebalance.

- If symptoms of motion sickness persist, take a longer break of a few days. Do not resume playing until feelings of dizziness are completely gone.

- Many users who initially have problems with motion sickness are able to eventually develop a tolerance.

VR environment. One drawback with this idea, however, is the way it limits players' freedom overall. Another idea is for the VR designer to create paths or tracks that help users visualize the direction of their next movement. In this way seeing the rails along which a VR roller coaster is hurtling would help users visualize the path they will take ahead of time, thus making the movement more predictable and less likely to cause motion sickness.

Yet another possibility is to slow things down in the virtual world. With the use of slow motion, fewer abrupt shifts of the camera, and less instances of acceleration and blurring effects, users feel more in control of the experience. In slow motion, gaudy effects such as lethal projectiles and flying debris in a crowded street scene are no longer disorienting. This makes users better able to predict movement in the VR environment and thus be less prone to motion sickness. Rather than wanting to throw up, users can relax and enjoy the stunning slow-motion effects.

Focusing on a Cockpit—or a Nose ■

One of the best ways for developers to reduce opportunities for motion sickness is to provide objects or visual cues as stable reference points to anchor viewers. Among the best objects for visual reference is a cockpit, control panel, or dashboard. It remains in place as a fixed item in a virtual world filled with objects in motion. Each time users let their eyes track back to the cockpit's controls, they can reorient themselves with the stable object as a reference point. Moreover, if a user's virtual avatar is seated in a cockpit, it helps if the user is also seated in the same position, creating a synchronization that makes movements in the VR world seem more predictable.

A tip from Olympic ice skaters can also help in this regard. As skaters spin, they focus on one point with each turn of their body. That is why skaters do not get dizzy coming out of blurring spins. The same rule holds true for navigating in virtual reality. If users keep their eyes focused on a single point while turning their head or rotating their body in a VR environment, they will avoid many risks of motion sickness.

Playing off this idea of a visual anchor, researchers at Purdue University have come up with their own solution. "We've discovered putting a virtual nose in the scene seems to have a stabilizing effect,"[42] says David Whittinghill, an assistant professor in Purdue University's Department of Computer Graphics Technology. According to Whittinghill, placing a cartoon nose where a viewer's nose would be, in the lower center of the headset screen, can reduce motion sickness by 13.5 percent. In a leisurely game exploring a Tuscan villa, users with the fake nose on the screen were able to play more than ninety seconds longer on average without feeling nauseated. Even on a stomach-churning roller-coaster game, the nose enabled users to last two seconds longer on average. "Our suspicion is that you have this stable object that your body is accustomed to tuning out, but it's still there and your sensory system knows it."[43]

Manipulating the Field of View ∎

Researchers at Columbia University are trying to help VR users avoid motion sickness without them even knowing it. Professors Steven Feiner and Ajoy Fernandes have learned they can significantly reduce motion sickness by subtly changing the VR users' FOV as they navigate the virtual world. They found that shrinking the FOV by masking the outer edges of the display can prevent users from growing nauseated and uncomfortable. The researchers have developed software that automatically reduces the FOV when the VR environment features a great deal of movement or the users themselves are moving. Fernandes, who suffers from VR

Emotional Hangover from Using VR

Tobias van Schneider is a dedicated player of Google's *Tilt Brush*. With his headset on, Van Schneider gains miraculous abilities as his fingertips paint streaks of colorful fire in the skies or mold the clouds into sculptures. When he tires of one created world, he can instantly leap into another one. But when he removes the headset, he finds himself back in his dreary, every-day existence. He can barely muster the energy to cope. "What stays is a strange feeling of sadness and disappointment when participating in the real world, usually on the same day," he wrote in an online blogging site. "The sky seems less colorful and it just feels like I'm missing the 'magic' (for lack of a better word). . . . I feel deeply disturbed and often end up just sitting there, staring at a wall."

As VR gaming grows, more users are also experiencing what Van Schneider calls post-VR sadness. After intensive sessions in virtual worlds, they come away feeling light-headed, detached, and unable to concentrate. The drabness of the real world compared to VR saps their emotional energy. Sometimes these effects linger for weeks or longer.

Some researchers believe these users suffer from an imbalance of serotonin, a chemical in the central nervous system that regulates mood swings. This condition also can affect the inner ear and produce dizziness and feelings of panic. Scientists say studies are needed to learn more about this troubling reaction to VR.

Quoted in Rebecca Searles, "Virtual Reality Can Leave You with an Existential Hangover," *Atlantic*, December 21, 2016. www.theatlantic.com.

sickness himself, got the idea from reading about change blindness, a psychological concept that examines why people often do not notice seemingly obvious changes in their surroundings. "So I wondered if this could be applied to VR," says Fernandes. "Could we change a participant's FOV without them noticing?"[44]

In a study with thirty volunteers, Feiner and Fernandes had the subjects walk, run, fly, or drive in their VR scenes while actually they were standing or sitting. The idea was to emphasize the sort of disjunction between physical motion cues and inner ear cues that can result in headaches and nausea. The subjects would use the FOV restrictors on the VR headsets one day and go without them the next. The restrictors were controlled by software that determined the extent of the FOV reduction and the length of time before the full view was restored. The trial showed that the subjects felt much better and were able to navigate the VR world longer with the FOV restrictors in use. If verified, the experiment indicates that concerns about tunnel vision in virtual reality set-ups may be unwarranted. "It is critical that the [VR] experience be both comfortable and compelling," says Feiner, "and we think we've found a way."[45]

Some scientists think the best way to address motion sickness is to expand the FOV, not contract it. Robert Xiao, of Carnegie Mellon's Human-Computer Interaction Institute, has added a low-cost array of light-emitting diodes (LEDs) to fill out the VR display to a wider horizon. The LEDs fill in what Xiao calls the VR headset's dark spots to add 60 degrees to the user's FOV. Xiao and his research partner Hrvoje Benko thought the added LEDs might address the problem of tunnel vision in consumer VR headsets but were surprised to find the LEDs also helped limit motion sickness for users. "You don't realize when you're playing with Oculus or other [headsets] how much black there really is in the device," says Xiao. "You strap it on, and the first thing your eyes focus on is the middle part, the bright screen. You

WORDS IN CONTEXT

restrictors

technology designed to confine or keep within certain specified limits or selected bounds

don't realize how much of the visual field is taken up by black, empty space."[46] Adding eighty strategically placed LEDs on the periphery of the display served to reduce feelings of dizziness and nausea and improve a player's overall awareness in the VR environment. Even though the LEDs are just glowing dots without real detail, they seem to help users orient themselves. The results startled Xiao and Benko because what available research there was suggested just the opposite would happen.

The test results at Columbia and Carnegie Mellon might seem contradictory. But mainly they demonstrate how individuals respond differently to VR and details like reduced or expanded FOV. Certainly much more research needs to be done in this area.

Avoiding Vision Problems with VR ■

More long-term studies also are needed with regard to VR's impact on users' eyes. Certainly, a prolonged period of staring at the screen inside a VR headset can lead to eyestrain. Because users tend to blink less when peering at a digital screen, the front surface of the eye can dry out and cause feelings of fatigue. For reasons of eye health, optometrists recommend that users limit their virtual reality sessions to a few minutes at a time, with frequent rest periods.

Concerns are more pronounced for children. VR companies like Oculus include health and safety warnings that headsets are not suitable for children under age thirteen. A few eye specialists have warned that children using headsets could develop double

A virtual reality enthusiast tries out the latest VR technology at a 2017 show in China. Prolonged periods of staring at the screen inside a VR headset can lead to eyestrain.

vision, which could lead to permanent eyesight problems. However, most ophthalmologists see no special dangers to children's eye development or vision health from using VR headsets. According to Stephen Lipsky, a pediatric ophthalmologist in Georgia, "Age limitations for VR technology might make sense for content, but as far as we know this technology poses no threat to the eyes."[47]

Eliminating a Visual Conflict ■

One eye problem associated with VR use is a condition called vergence-accommodation conflict. Staring at a very close stereoscopic display, which presents the left and right eye with slightly different images in order to simulate depth, causes the eyes to constantly adjust their focus, creating a conflict between where they are looking and where they are focused. This can lead to significant eye fatigue. Now scientists at the University of Illinois at Urbana-Champaign have developed a new VR display module that addresses this conflict. Using a technology called optical mapping near eye, highly realistic three-dimensional images can be generated with a series of four 2D subpanel images. Although the display is extremely close to the eyes, as in commercial VR headsets, it creates depth cues for natural focus just as in the real world. Since where the eyes are pointing and where they are focused is matched, the vergence-accommodation conflict is almost nil.

The team worked with a black-and-white demonstration video of parked cars shot close to and far away from the cars. The team was able to create depth perception in a new way that nonetheless conformed to the way the human eye perceives depth. Although the new display modules must be reduced in size and weight, the team hopes soon to partner with VR firms for mass production.

Virtual reality may never be suitable for all people, as susceptibility to problems such as motion sickness varies widely. However, with VR innovations appearing more and more frequently, the technology promises to make a huge impact on society and culture in the future.

SOURCE NOTES

INTRODUCTION
Virtual Treatment for Real Phobias

1. Jessica Vitkus, "Why You Should Care—Because Fear Should Never Hold You Back," *Ozy*, March 16, 2017. www.ozy.com.
2. Quoted in Cornell Tech, "The Challenges and Possibilities of Virtual Reality Startups," March 8, 2016. https://tech.cornell.edu.

CHAPTER 1
CURRENT STATUS: A Simulated World

3. Quoted in Jack Money, "Virtual Reality Arcade Coming to Penn Square Mall in Oklahoma City," *Oklahoman* (Oklahoma City, OK), November 15, 2016. http://newsok.com.
4. Quoted in Money, "Virtual Reality Arcade Coming to Penn Square Mall in Oklahoma City."
5. Quoted in Tim Bradshaw, "VR Industry Faces Reality Check on Sales Growth," *Financial Times*, February 28, 2017. www.ft.com.
6. Quoted in Niall Firth, "Virtual Reality: Meet Founding Father Jaron Lanier," *New Scientist*, June 19, 2013. www.newscientist.com.
7. Quoted in Bruce Sterling, "Augmented Reality: 'The Ultimate Display' by Ivan Sutherland, 1965," *Wired*, September 20, 2009. www.wired.com.
8. Quoted in NASA Science, "Whatever Happened to Virtual Reality?," November 11, 2004. https://science.nasa.gov.
9. Dan Seitz, "Twenty Years Later, Let's Remember the Virtual Boy Failure That Saved Nintendo," Uproxx, July 21, 2015. http://uproxx.com.
10. Matthew Schnipper, "Seeing Is Believing: The State of Virtual Reality," Verge. www.theverge.com.

11. Andy O'Donnell, "Is Your PC Ready for Virtual Reality?," Lifewire, December 12, 2016. www.lifewire.com.
12. Quoted in Mark Pesce, "Virtual Reality Is Actually Made of Smartphones," *Register*, October 13, 2016. www.theregister .co.uk.
13. Pesce, "Virtual Reality Is Actually Made of Smartphones."
14. Christopher Mims, "Why the Virtual-Reality Hype Is About to Come Crashing Down," *Wall Street Journal*, May 23, 2016. www.wsj.com.

CHAPTER 2
PROBLEMS: Getting a Sense of Being There

15. Quoted in Rod Chester, "Health Warning as Immersive Virtual Reality Craze Linked to Vision Problems," News.com.au, February 25, 2017. www.news.com.au.
16. Quoted in Dan Crawley, "We're Not Talking About What VR Is Doing to Our Eyes . . . and Our Brains," VentureBeat, April 18, 2015. https://venturebeat.com.
17. Michael Abrash, "Latency—the *Sine Qua Non* of AR and VR," *Ramblings in Valve Time* (blog), December 29, 2012. http:// blogs.valvesoftware.com.
18. Alex Colgan, "4 Ways to Unleash the Power of Sound in VR," *Leap Motion* (blog), April 17, 2015. http://blog.leapmotion .com.
19. Virtual Reality Society, "Getting to Grips with Haptic Technology," 2017. www.vrs.org.uk.
20. Chet Faliszek, @chetfaliszek, Twitter, July 8, 2016. https:// mobile.twitter.com.
21. Brian, @PS4_Trophies, Twitter, October 13, 2016. https:// mobile.twitter.com.
22. Quoted in Betsy Mason, "Virtual Reality Has a Motion Sickness Problem," *Science News*, March 7, 2017. www.science news.org.
23. leppermessiah1,"VR Land Sickness aka VR Hangover aka Mal de Debarquement Syndrome," Reddit: PlayStation VR, October 19, 2016. www.reddit.com.

CHAPTER 3
SOLUTIONS: Achieving and Maintaining Presence

24. Sasa Marinkovic, "First Rule of VR: Don't Break the Presence," TechCrunch, February 7, 2015. https://techcrunch.com.

25. Marinkovic, "First Rule of VR."

26. Ben Lang, "Hands-On: The New and Improved StarVR Prototype Will Give You Field-of-View Envy," Road to VR, June 17, 2016. www.roadtovr.com.

27. Yuval Boger (VRGuy), "Understanding Pixel Density and Eye-Limiting Resolution," *The VRguy's Blog*, Sensics, June 6, 2016. http://sensics.com.

28. Quoted in Ben Lang, "Eonite Claims to Have Solved Inside-Out Positional Tracking for VR and AR," Road to VR, January 12, 2017. www.roadtovr.com.

29. Quoted in Ben Kuchera, "The Complete Guide to Virtual Reality in 2016 (So Far)," Polygon, January 15, 2016. www.polygon.com.

30. Quoted in IEEE Xplore, "Humanizing VR Part 3: How Photorealistic Should a 3D Virtual Human Be?," June 3, 2016. http://ieeexplore-spotlight.ieee.org.

31. Quoted in Rachel Metz, "People in Virtual Reality Are About to Look a Lot More Realistic," *MIT Technology Review*, March 14, 2016. www.technologyreview.com.

CHAPTER 4
SOLUTIONS: Appealing to the Senses

32. Quoted in Steve Dent, "Researchers Simulate Walls in VR by Shocking Your Muscles," *Engadget* (blog), April 17, 2017. www.engadget.com.

33. Quoted in Dent, "Researchers Simulate Walls in VR by Shocking Your Muscles."

34. Paul James, "'Teslasuit' Kickstarter Is Live, Full Body Haptic Suits Start at £119," Road to VR, January 4, 2016. www.roadtovr.com.

35. Jamie Rigg, "Teslasuit Does Full-Body Haptic Feedback for VR," *Engadget* (blog), January 6, 2016. www.engadget.com.

36. Ryan Whitwam, "This Exoskeleton Glove Could Let You Feel the 'Shape' of Virtual Reality," *Extreme Tech* (blog), August 26, 2016. www.extremetech.com.

37. Quoted in Simon Parkin, "This Accessory Makes VR So Real a Surgeon Could Train with It," *MIT Technology Review*, September 30, 2016. www.technologyreview.com.

38. Adi Robertson, "Smellovision Masks Are Here, and They're Basically Implements of Torture," Verge, March 6, 2015. www.theverge.com.

39. Quoted in Gillian Mohney, "Digital 'Lollipop' Will Zap Tongue with Flavor," ABC News, November 25, 2013. http://abcnews.go.com.

40. Quoted in Victoria Turk, "Face Electrodes Let You Taste and Chew in Virtual Reality," *New Scientist*, November 4, 2016. www.newscientist.com.

CHAPTER 5
SOLUTIONS: Reducing Motion Sickness

41. Sarah Zhang, "The Neuroscience of Why VR Still Sucks," Gizmodo, March 18, 2015. https://gizmodo.com.

42. Quoted in Liz Stinson, "How to Reduce VR Sickness? Just Add a Virtual Nose," *Wired*, April 20, 2015. www.wired.com.

43. Quoted in Stephanie Pappas, "Why Does Virtual Reality Make Some People Sick?," Live Science, April 20, 2016. www.livescience.com.

44. Quoted in Debra Kaufman, "Study Shows Restricting Field of View Alleviates VR Sickness," *ETCentric*, June 20, 2016. www.etcentric.org.

45. Quoted in Kaufman, "Study Shows Restricting Field of View Alleviates VR Sickness."

46. Quoted in Sam Machkovech, "How Side-Mounted LEDs Can Help Fix VR's 'Tunnel Vision' and Nausea Problems," Ars Technica, May 9, 2016. https://arstechnica.com.

47. Quoted in Reena Mukamal, "Are Virtual Reality Headsets Safe for Eyes?," American Academy of Ophthalmology, February 28, 2017. www.aao.org.

Books

Holly Clark et al., *The Google Cardboard Book: Explore, Engage, and Educate with Virtual Reality*. Irvine, CA: EdTechTeam, 2017.

Bradley Austin Davis and Karen Bryla, *Oculus Rift in Action*. New York: Manning, 2015.

Philippe Fuchs and Guillaume Moreau, *Virtual Reality: Concepts and Technologies*. London: Taylor & Francis Group, 2011.

Jason Jerald, *The VR Book: Human-Centered Design for Virtual Reality*. Williston, VT: Morgan & Claypool, 2016.

Tony Parisi, *Learning Virtual Reality: Developing Immersive Experiences and Applications for Desktop, Web, and Mobile*. Sebastopol, CA: O'Reilly Media, 2016.

Internet Sources

Sophie Charara, "Explained: How Does VR Actually Work?," *Wareable*, May 22, 2017. www.wareable.com/vr/how-does-vr-work-explained.

Ben Lang, "Oculus Shares 5 Key Ingredients for Presence in Virtual Reality," *Road to VR*, September 24, 2014. www.roadtovr.com/oculus-shares-5-key-ingredients-for-presence-in-virtual-reality.

Betsy Mason, "Virtual Reality Has a Motion Sickness Problem," *Science News*, March 7, 2017. www.sciencenews.org/article/virtual-reality-has-motion-sickness-problem.

Mark Pesce, "Virtual Reality Is Actually Made of Smartphones," *Register*, October 13, 2016. www.theregister.co.uk/2016/10/13/virtual_reality_is_made_of_smartphones.

Andrew Zalewski, "VR, Simulation Are New Frontiers of Surgical Training Outside OR," MedCity News, August 31, 2016. http://medcitynews.com/2016/08/vr-surgical-simulation-training.

Websites

Infinity Leap (https://infinityleap.com). This cutting-edge website features the latest news and discussions about developments in virtual reality and augmented reality. Stories cover applications for VR in entertainment, gaming, medicine, business, and many other areas.

TechCrunch (https://techcrunch.com). TechCrunch is a media website dedicated to breaking tech news, with an emphasis on virtual reality. It includes articles and news stories on VR by dedicated tech geeks and bloggers.

Virtual Reality Society (www.vrs.org.uk). This website offers an excellent overview of topics related to virtual reality, including "What Is Virtual Reality?," "Who Invented Virtual Reality?," and "Assessment of Virtual Reality Systems."

VR Dribble (www.vrdribble.com). With the goal to integrate virtual reality into people's lives, this website is an online platform providing news, reviews, and the latest developments in VR and AR.

INDEX

ABOUT THE AUTHOR

John Allen is a writer who lives and works in Oklahoma City.